SHELTERS
From Tepee to Igloo

Also by Harvey Weiss

Machines and How They Work

Hammer and Saw
An Introduction to Woodworking

How to Be an Inventor

How to Make Your Own Books

How to Run a Railroad
Everything You Need to Know About Model Trains

Model Airplanes and How to Build Them

Model Buildings and How to Build Them

Model Cars and Trucks and How to Build Them

Motors and Engines and How They Work

SHELTERS

From Tepee to Igloo

Harvey Weiss

Thomas Y. Crowell   New York

Shelters: From Tepee to Igloo
Copyright © 1988 by Harvey Weiss
Printed in the U.S.A. All rights reserved.

Library of Congress Cataloging-in-Publication Data
Weiss, Harvey.
  Shelters, from teepee to igloo.

  Summary: Describes a number of shelters constructed
from different types of materials and suitable to
varying climates, including tepees, yurts, log cabins,
stone houses, and igloos.
  1. Dwellings—Juvenile literature. [1. Dwellings]
I. Title.
GT172.W45 1988   392′.36   87-47698
ISBN 0-690-04553-0
ISBN 0-690-04555-7 (lib. bdg.)

1 2 3 4 5 6 7 8 9 10
First Edition

Contents

SHELTERS

From Tepee to Igloo

Introduction

Houses take many forms. The sort of house that most of us live in has a roof and four walls. Or you may live in an apartment that is one part of a larger building. These are the usual sort of dwellings that we are comfortable and familiar with. But there are many other kinds.

Some are common—such as tents. Others are strange and exotic and found in distant lands—such as yurts! In case you don't know, a yurt is a sort of squat tepee favored by Mongolian tribespeople. It is framed with many thin wood strips, covered with felt, and likely to leak when it rains.

This book is about the many different forms that dwellings take. It is about the shelters that people make who don't live in modern towns or cities. It is about where they are built, who builds them, and why they take the form that they do.

The sort of "house" people live in is determined by two things. One is the needs of the people who live there. Do they need to keep warm? Or cool? Do they have to move

often? Do they need to erect their dwelling fast? Do they have to be protected from hostile forces outside? Do they have to build it with simple tools and unskilled labor?

The second thing that determines the form a dwelling takes is the materials available. In a land where there is lots of rock and stone, chances are this is what will be used. Where there is snow and ice, we find the igloo. A builder will make use of mud and clay where there is nothing else. And when a shelter is needed in or near

forests, the material used will, no doubt, be wood.

Some of the shelters described here are not built anymore. Some are primitive (or, at least, very simple), although one—the geodesic dome—is as modern as tomorrow. But all these dwellings are interesting to know about because they tell us something about the people who built them, the materials they had to work with, and the sort of world they lived in.

Igloos

The Eskimo people live in the northern part of the North American continent and in northeast Asia. These are cold, barren lands where farming or cattle raising is not possible. The Eskimos live by hunting and fishing, and so the most important and respected Eskimos are the most skilled hunters and fishermen.

In order to get to the best hunting and fishing places at the right time of year, the Eskimos move about a good deal. In summer they often live in tents. Some of the

14

tents are made with wooden poles and animal skins. Some are store-bought canvas tents.

In winter an Eskimo dwelling is another matter altogether. Blizzards, endless snow, and extremely cold weather make for living conditions so difficult, it is sometimes hard to understand how families can survive. But they do. One of the reasons they manage to survive—with security and comfort—is that they know how to build igloos.

When possible, the igloo builder makes the entrance tunnel slant downhill, as shown here. This keeps the warm air from leaking out.

The igloo is always placed so that the entrance faces away from the prevailing winds.

The raised "shelves" in igloos provide comfortable places for sitting or sleeping. Because warm air rises, these shelves are warmer than the igloo floor.

In the Eskimo language the word *igloo* means any kind of shelter. That includes a tent or a driftwood house or a shelter built of stone. And Eskimos in different northern climate areas do live in many different kinds of shelters. But most people think of only one kind of shelter when the word igloo is used. They think of the domed constructions built of blocks of snow, like the one shown here.

An igloo won't ever be the same temperature as a steam-heated apartment. But then, Eskimos, who are used to living in a cold environment, wouldn't want it that warm. The reason an igloo stays at a livable temperature is that the snow acts as an insulator: it keeps heat inside, and it keeps out wind and cold air.

The body heat from two or three people in an igloo keeps the temperature high enough for comfort, even without a fire. A small camp stove will make a well-built igloo almost warm—or at least somewhat warmer than freezing. If an igloo got too warm, the snow blocks would begin to melt.

When an Eskimo family is on the move, they can put together a small "overnight" igloo in little more than an hour. A large, carefully built igloo that a large family intends to live in for some time will take much longer to build.

There are very definite rules and procedures for building an igloo. First a circle about ten feet in diameter is marked out. Then blocks of snow measuring about one by two by three feet are cut. The thickness of the block is determined by the kind of snow being used. If the snow is hard packed, a thinner block can be used. If the snow is less compacted, a thicker block is needed. If the snow is loose and fluffy, blocks can't be cut at all and an igloo can't be built.

The snow blocks are laid down in spiral form. The blocks in the first row gradually increase in size. The rest of the blocks are shaped so that they lean inward. The spiral is completed at the very top of the igloo.

knife for cutting the blocks of snow

Tepees

The tepee is a practically designed dwelling that was ideally suited to the needs of the American Plains Indians. These tribes were dependent on buffalo. Because the buffalo roamed, so did the Indians. This called for a shelter, such as the tepee, that could be easily moved.

The buffalo provided not only food for the Indians but also hides, which were used as coverings for the tepees. A large tepee might need twenty or more hides. They were sewn together and draped over long poles. When the Indians wanted to move to a new hunting ground, it was fairly simple to fold the cover into a compact bundle and bring it along.

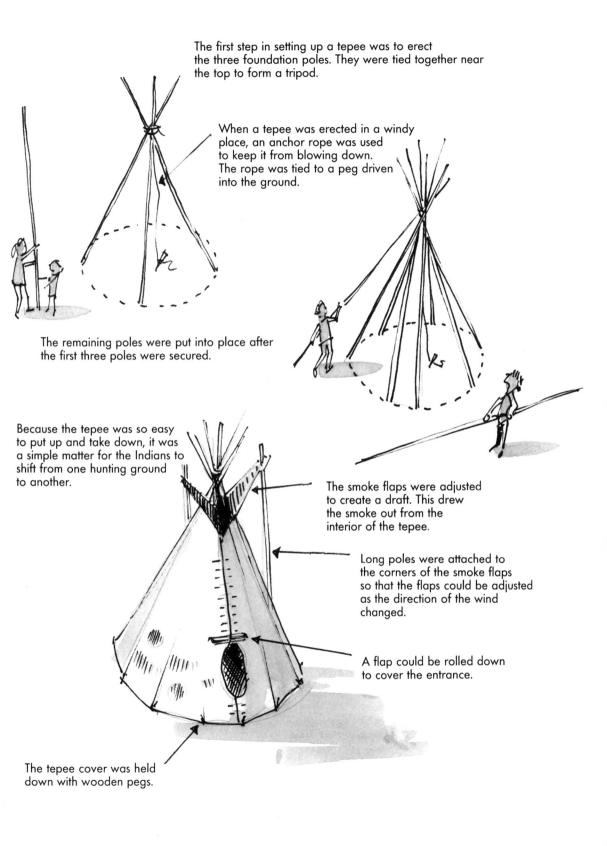

The first step in setting up a tepee was to erect the three foundation poles. They were tied together near the top to form a tripod.

When a tepee was erected in a windy place, an anchor rope was used to keep it from blowing down. The rope was tied to a peg driven into the ground.

The remaining poles were put into place after the first three poles were secured.

Because the tepee was so easy to put up and take down, it was a simple matter for the Indians to shift from one hunting ground to another.

The smoke flaps were adjusted to create a draft. This drew the smoke out from the interior of the tepee.

Long poles were attached to the corners of the smoke flaps so that the flaps could be adjusted as the direction of the wind changed.

A flap could be rolled down to cover the entrance.

The tepee cover was held down with wooden pegs.

The Indians had an interesting way of moving heavy loads such as this. They used something called a *travois*. Two long poles were hitched to a dog or horse. The load was lashed to the poles, which were dragged along the ground. Originally only dogs were used for this purpose, but they could pull only small loads. Matters were simplified somewhat when the Indians began using horses. (The Indians didn't always have horses. The Spanish first brought them to Mexico and the Plains Indians acquired them in the eighteenth century.)

The travois was perfectly suited to the Indian environment. There were no roads or trails, and the travois worked well in all kinds of wild terrain where a wagon would have had trouble passing. The one big difficulty with the travois was that the poles quickly wore down

This is a travois.

Children could ride on top of a bundled-up tepee cover. It was also possible to arrange a platform to carry infants or the aged. Even with springy poles, however, this must have been a very bouncy ride.

from being dragged along the ground for long distances. And strong, straight poles weren't always easy to find. A good set of poles might be worth as much as a horse.

Tepees were ingeniously constructed so that the interior could be cleared of smoke. Indian families always kept a fire going in the tepee for cooking or, in winter, for heat. Tepees had a pair of smoke flaps, which directed the wind in such a way that it drew smoke out. By moving the flaps around, the Indians could control the draft. In snow or rain, the flaps could be completely closed.

In very cold weather a temporary fence of brush was sometimes put up as a windbreak. The door flap was closed to keep in the heat from the fire.

Another way to keep the tepee warm was to hang a layer of buffalo skins along the inside of the tepee cover. This insulating layer kept drafts out and heat in.

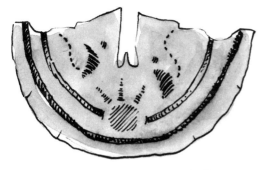

Buffalo hides were sewn together to make the tepee cover. This is how the cover looked when spread out flat.

Horses and buffalo were very important to the Indians of the Plains and appeared frequently in tepee designs.

The designs were often a record of various important events. For example, they might show a battle fought, or a hunting expedition.

The designs on the tepee coverings were often dramatic and quite beautiful.

Indians who lived in other climates and in different environments built many other kinds of dwellings. In forests they stretched large pieces of bark over bent poles to make snug, weatherproof dwellings called wigwams. In the forests of the northeastern and northwestern United States, Indians lived in solid buildings made of wood planks. In parts of the Southwest, they used mud and clay bricks to make adobe houses, which are described on pages 36 to 41.

Indians who didn't travel and who lived in northern, more heavily forested climates built shelters using saplings and thin, flexible poles.

The same kind of bent-pole arrangement is found in shelters of many different lands. However, the covering varies, depending on what is locally available—anything from felt to cloth to thatch.

The poles were tied together to make a support that looked like an upside-down basket.

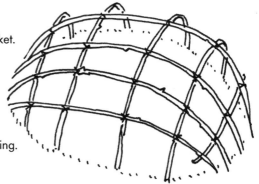

The bent-pole structure was covered with bark from birch trees. This kind of bark can be peeled off in large, wide strips and makes an excellent covering. (It is the same kind of bark used to make birch-bark canoes.)

A hole in the top let the smoke out.

The bark was laced or sewn into place.

Some North American Indians called these structures wigwams. A large wigwam might have had bark roofing and a different material for the walls.

Yurts

Do you yearn for a yurt? Probably not. Nevertheless, it is an important and interesting kind of shelter well worth a good look. It has been used since the time of Genghis Khan (who lived in the 1200's) and it is still used by many people in parts of Russia, Mongolia, and Siberia.

A yurt is a little like a tepee because both consist of a thin wood frame covered with a weather-resistant material. But the yurt has a low wall that supports the roof poles. This wall gives it a low, rounded shape that can withstand strong winds.

The yurt is self-supporting. It doesn't need ropes or stakes or poles driven into the ground. This is important, because where the yurt is used, on the central Asian steppes, the ground is often frozen hard as a rock.

The peoples who use the yurt are mostly shepherds. They raise sheep and goats, and as the grazing land becomes used up they must shift camp, seeking new pastures. Their lifestyle is not unlike that of the American Plains Indians, who were always moving in search of

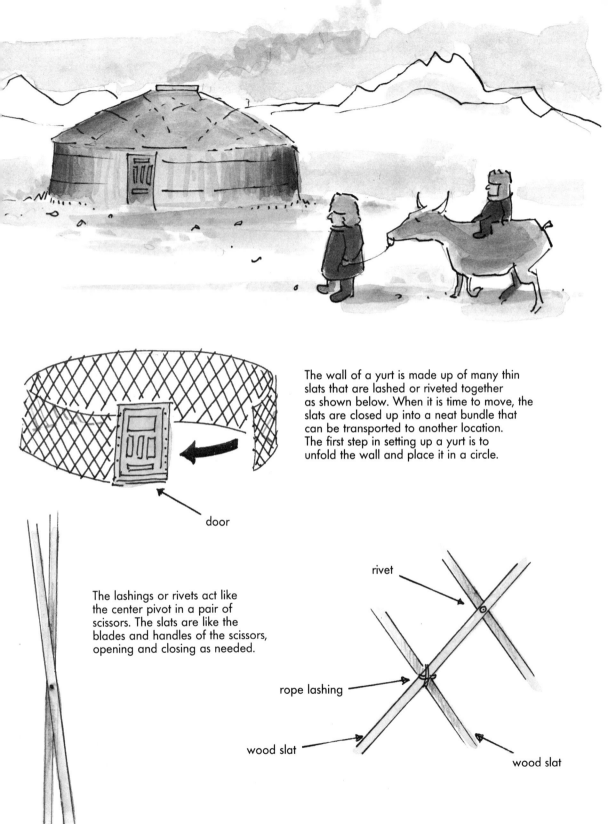

The wall of a yurt is made up of many thin slats that are lashed or riveted together as shown below. When it is time to move, the slats are closed up into a neat bundle that can be transported to another location. The first step in setting up a yurt is to unfold the wall and place it in a circle.

door

The lashings or rivets act like the center pivot in a pair of scissors. The slats are like the blades and handles of the scissors, opening and closing as needed.

rivet

rope lashing

wood slat

wood slat

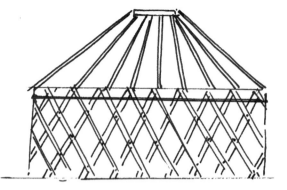

This is the basic structure of a yurt, with the roof frame in place.

The top of the yurt has a ring called a crown. The roof poles are attached to it. The crown is open in the center. It lets in light and lets out smoke from the heating and cooking fire.

buffalo. The Indians were hunters, though; the yurt dwellers are shepherds.

A yurt is portable like a tent. When the shepherds want to move, they remove the roof cover and bundle it up. Next they take down the roof poles, fold up the walls, and pack everything on the backs of one or two yaks or camels. (A yak is a long-haired ox found in parts of central Asia.)

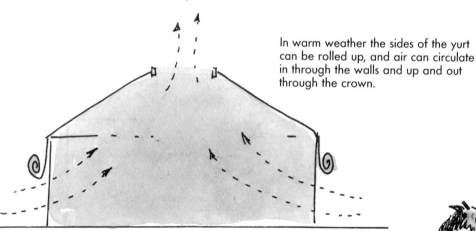

In warm weather the sides of the yurt can be rolled up, and air can circulate in through the walls and up and out through the crown.

Because the yurt dwellers are shepherds, they have plenty of sheep to provide wool for the felt coverings.

The construction of a yurt is quite difficult. The various parts have to be designed to fit well and support the weight of the cover. The covers of Mongolian yurts are made of felt. Felt is a weighty, bulky material. In very cold weather several layers are used.

A number of people in the United States have fallen in love with this kind of house and developed different variations of it using modern methods and materials. Quite a few yurts have been built in rural areas of New England, where they have been part of educational programs exploring alternate living styles. The yurts have turned out to be snug and pleasant under even the coldest winter conditions.

Yurts constructed with modern materials have been built in many places. They have proved to be practical and comfortable in even the harshest winter conditions.

Log Cabins

The first houses built of logs—log cabins—were made in Scandinavia and northern Germany, where trees were plentiful. The early settlers in America lived in log cabins because they were quick and easy to build. Putting up a log cabin didn't require many tools or great skill. A log is a simple material. It is just a piece of tree. It doesn't have to be sawed into boards or timbers. It just has to be cut to the right length with the odd branches chopped off. When trees were cut down to clear the land for farming, a plentiful supply of the raw material was there for the taking.

Some of the early log buildings were in Russia and Siberia, where there was a plentiful supply of wood. They were simple, square structures, and their size was determined by the logs available to build them.

The roofs were often made of sod—earth and grass—which was placed on top of a wooden structure. Over the years the dirt became compact, dense, and waterproof.

Early settlers in North America were accomplishing two things when they cut down the trees in the forests: They were opening up the land, making fields where crops could be raised. At the same time they were gathering the logs they needed to build their dwellings. Actually, getting rid of the tree stumps was more difficult than cutting down the trees.

The logs were fitted together with notches. Nails weren't needed. One log fitted onto another with no chance of slipping. The notches provided a ridged and strong means of attachment, and they could be cut with a fair degree of accuracy using nothing more than a sharp axe.

The thick log walls acted as a good insulator, keeping a well-built log cabin cool in summer and warm in winter.

When notched like this, one log will fit snugly against the adjoining one.

Gaps between the logs were sealed with moss and dried grass mixed with mud or clay.

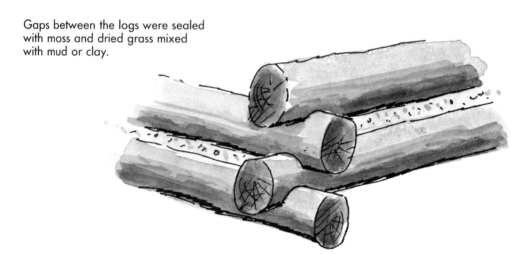

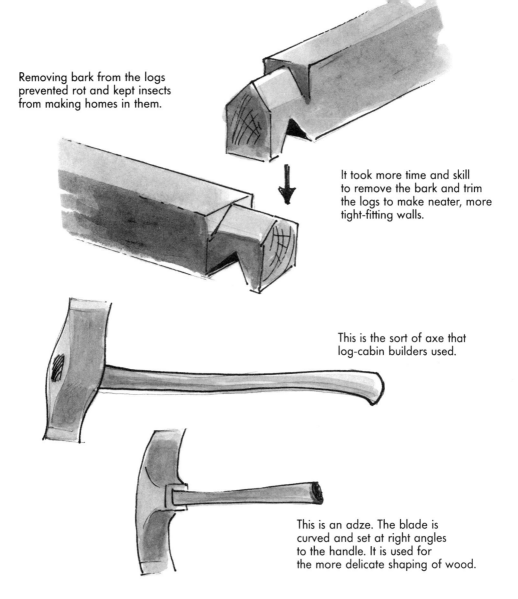

Removing bark from the logs prevented rot and kept insects from making homes in them.

It took more time and skill to remove the bark and trim the logs to make neater, more tight-fitting walls.

This is the sort of axe that log-cabin builders used.

This is an adze. The blade is curved and set at right angles to the handle. It is used for the more delicate shaping of wood.

The settlers mixed clay with grass, moss, or straw and jammed it between the logs to seal the cracks.

These primitive log cabins were rather dark inside, because it was a tricky business to make a workable window. Besides, most early settlers were in dangerous country, and the log cabin might have to be defended

31

against attack. Too many windows would have made defense difficult.

Glass was not available, and so sometimes the settlers used oiled paper. In warm weather they left the windows open. Wooden shutters were used in bad weather.

There are, of course, many variations of the log cabin. The early cabins, built in the 1600's and 1700's, were crude. But when more tools and skilled carpenters came on the scene, the log cabins became larger and fancier. Some were built with several rooms, two or more fireplaces, and even a second story. Different materials were used for the roofs, although cedar shingles were used wherever possible. Sometimes roofs were made of boards caulked with moss and grass. Sometimes half-log slabs were used. In the 1800's corrugated tin first appeared and became popular.

The shingles were nailed onto a beam-and-board framework something like this.

Cedar shingles were often used for the roof. Today cedar shingles are sometimes used for the outside walls as well as for the roof.

Because cedar trees have a straight grain, and are easy to split and resistant to rot, they make the ideal shingle.

The fireplace was built from large stones. The chimney was constructed of sticks and lined with mud or clay.

Most modern houses have wooden frameworks to which walls are attached both inside and outside. The log cabin was much simpler. It didn't require any supporting framework to hold up the walls. The logs were both framework and wall.

This is the way the early settler made shingles. He used a heavy hammer and a froe, which is like a very wide, sharp chisel with a handle.

These are some of the materials that were used at various times to roof log cabins:

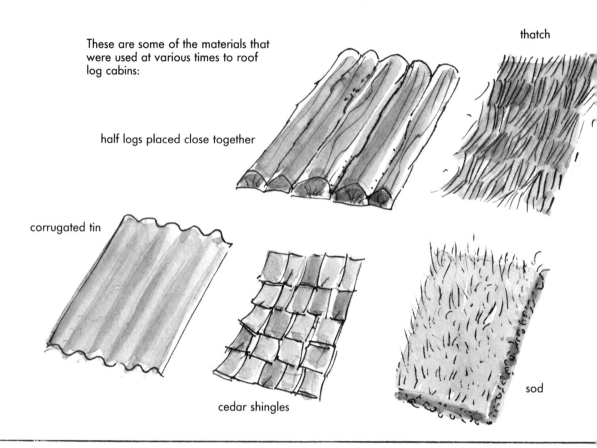

thatch

half logs placed close together

corrugated tin

cedar shingles

sod

When there is a plentiful supply of wood, many kinds of shelter can be easily and quickly assembled. They may be lifesavers in sudden bad weather.

Trees fallen against a steep hillside can provide temporary shelter for a backpacker caught in a rain- or snowstorm.

A rather peculiar variation of the log cabin was built in the United States in the early 1900's by the laborers who worked on the railroads. Railroad ties were plentiful and could be used to make crude, temporary shelters.

Adobe Dwellings

For people who live in a very dry, hot part of the world such as northern Africa or Mexico, where there is not much stone or wood, the earth itself provides the material for building—a mixture of earth, straw, and clay. The earth-straw-clay is mixed with water to make it pliable. Then the mixture is jammed into molds that shape the bricks. The bricks are removed from the molds and dried in the sun. When they are dry and hard, they are assembled into walls. The walls are usually plastered over with a layer of mud or clay.

A form or mold is used to shape the brick. A simple wood construction like this is one kind of form often used.

After the form is filled and the mixture packed down, the form is disassembled so the brick can dry out.

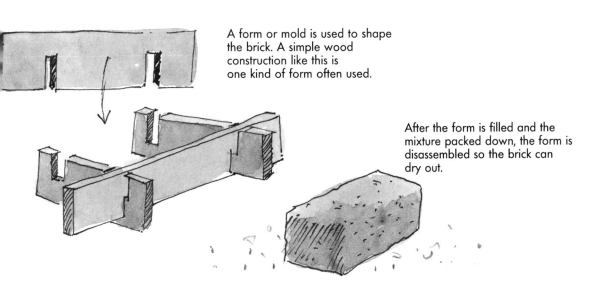

In Mali, in West Africa, some adobe structures have wood projections that serve as permanent scaffolds. If the walls need fixing, it is a simple matter to climb up and make the necessary repairs.

The flat roof of an adobe house provides an open area—an outdoor living room—where the family often gathers once the sun has set.

Since adobe buildings are built in places where there is little rain, and certainly no snow, the roofs can be quite flat. Wood poles, called rafters, run from the top of one wall to another. Twigs and dried grass are spread over the rafters, and a layer of earth-straw-clay is spread on top. In many climates the flat roof is vital because it collects rainwater, sometimes the only water available. The water drains off the roof and is stored in large underground cisterns. If a little sand or mud gets mixed in with the water during a rainstorm, it isn't really a problem. As the water sits in the storage tank, the impurities sink to the bottom, leaving clean water on top.

This is a cutaway view of adobe roof construction.

The top surface is the adobe mix.

Heavy poles serve as roof rafters.

twigs and straw on top of rafters

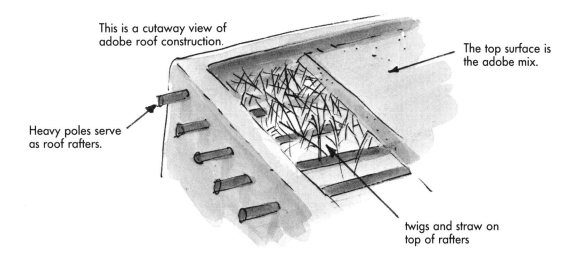

A clay or metal spout is placed at the edge of the roof so that rainwater will quickly drain off.

adobe mix

straw and brush

roof rafter

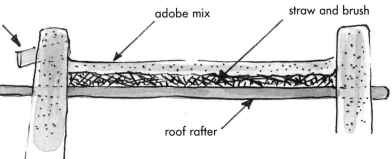

Sometimes other materials, such as roots, gravel, or pot shards, are added to the usual adobe mixture. Each community has its own adobe formula, which is often a carefully guarded secret.

Because the walls are thick, the windows are always deep set.

An adobe wall is often plastered over with a liquid adobe mixture and then whitewashed to reflect the sun.

The Pueblo Indians of New Mexico are known for the communities of adobe houses they built during the nineteenth century. Often one adobe house was built on top of another until a many-storied "apartment house" resulted.

In many dry, undeveloped countries adobe houses are still built. The method of construction hasn't changed much. But in more sophisticated designs various chemicals are added to the adobe brick to make it tougher and more weather resistant. Some modern adobe houses have all the conveniences found in any other kind of contemporary home.

Originally Pueblo Indian houses were built close together and even on top of one another for better protection against attacks by hostile tribes.

In some areas of Africa houses are built by piling up handfuls of a mud-clay-grass mixture. Because the climate is very hot and dry, the mixture dries as it is applied. The roof is usually made of thatch.

On page 55 there is an explanation of how a thatched roof is made.

Bedouin Tents

In many parts of northern Africa and Asia, and especially in the deserts of Arab countries, there are people with no permanent dwelling. They are Bedouins. The land these nomads wander through is arid and inhospitable. There isn't enough rain or the proper soil to make farming possible. The livelihood of the Bedouins is provided

by the sheep, goats, and camels that they raise. The camel is particularly important. It provides meat and milk. Camel wool is used for clothing, camel dung is used for fuel, and camel skin provides footwear and water bags. In a really dire emergency a camel can be slaughtered and a traveler about to die of thirst can drink the stomach fluid.

The Bedouins dwell in tents. They are called black tents because they are usually woven from black goat hair. These tents are made up of many strips sewn together, and they are quite heavy. The Bedouins can use this kind of tent only because they have camels to carry them from one place to another.

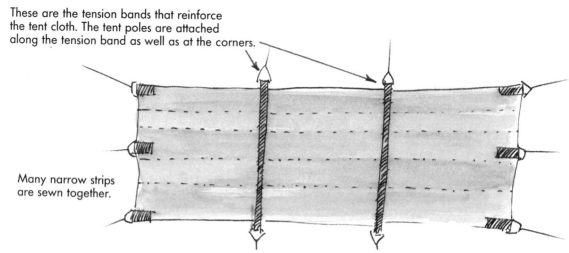

These are the tension bands that reinforce the tent cloth. The tent poles are attached along the tension band as well as at the corners.

Many narrow strips are sewn together.

Goat hair is most suitable for this kind of tent because it is strong and doesn't stretch. Camel hair or sheep wool is good-looking but won't make quite as rugged a fabric as goat hair.

A black tent is rectangular. It is definitely not the kind of tent a backpacker would carry on a hike along the Appalachian Trail. The corners are heavily reinforced and a strip of strong fabric called a tension band is sewn across the middle. The tent is held up by a series of poles. The poles are placed so that the tent is almost flat. This keeps the wind from getting a grip on it and blowing it away. Ropes are stretched out as shown in the drawing.

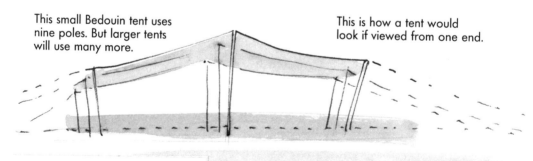

This small Bedouin tent uses nine poles. But larger tents will use many more.

This is how a tent would look if viewed from one end.

Wood is scarce in desert lands, so tent poles are quite valuable.

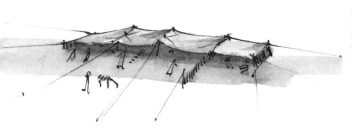

The Bedouin tent is a place where all travelers and visitors are received and offered food and shelter. Even uninvited or unwelcome guests, according to tradition and unwritten law, are provided with at least three days of hospitality.

They go out a long way in order to provide the maximum tension. The end of each rope is tied around a bush and buried in the sand. (Or the ropes can be attached to stakes driven deep into the sand.) The long ropes have another purpose—to trip up an enemy raider approaching on a horse or camel, giving the tent dweller time for defensive action.

The Bedouin tent comes in many sizes. A wealthy Arab with many camels and a large household might have a tent seventy feet long and twenty or more feet wide. The loom that the tent dweller uses produces a long strip of fabric. These strips are sewn together to make the tent. The more strips side by side, the wider the tent. The longer the strips, the longer the tent.

In hot weather the tent is left open to whatever breezes happen to be blowing. When the weather is cold or when sand is blowing, wall curtains are pinned to the edge of the tent. Additional curtains can be placed elsewhere for privacy. Normal daytime activity, however, is pretty much out of doors and the tent functions mainly as a large and elaborate sunshade.

One kind of curtain is always put up in the Bedouin tent. It is called a dividing curtain. This curtain keeps

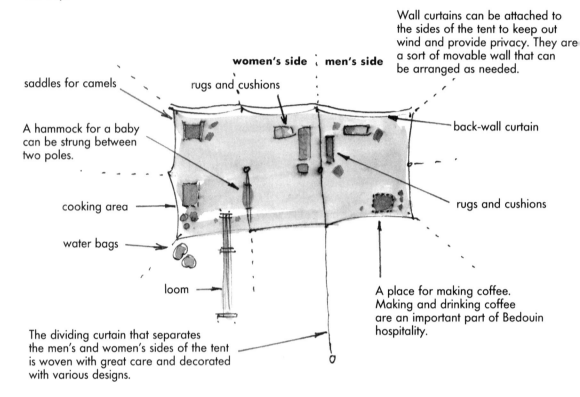

The interior of a Bedouin tent would probably be arranged this way.

Wall curtains can be attached to the sides of the tent to keep out wind and provide privacy. They are a sort of movable wall that can be arranged as needed.

women's side   **men's side**

saddles for camels

rugs and cushions

A hammock for a baby can be strung between two poles.

back-wall curtain

cooking area

rugs and cushions

water bags

loom

A place for making coffee. Making and drinking coffee are an important part of Bedouin hospitality.

The dividing curtain that separates the men's and women's sides of the tent is woven with great care and decorated with various designs.

the women doing the weaving and cooking and housekeeping tasks in their section of the tent while the men drink lots of coffee and engage in serious, "manly" conversations!

There are many variations on the flat Bedouin tent. Different pole arrangements, different coverings and different shapes and sizes have developed wherever there are nomad tribes. For example, the tent style in Afghanistan is quite different from that of the Iranian or Pakistani nomad. This is only to be expected, because the needs of all people and the materials available will never be exactly the same.

46

connector

In Morocco the tent has a different arrangement of supports, with two center poles joined by a short connector.

The Moroccan tent has a hump like a camel.

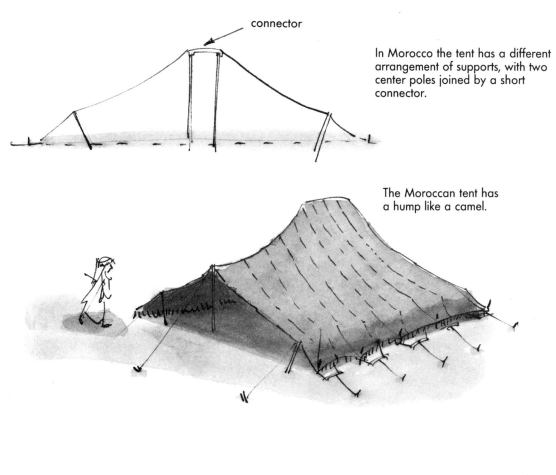

Camels are used to carry the tents from one place to another.

Japanese Houses

Japan is one of the world's most modern countries. It has large industrial centers and cities such as Tokyo, Osaka, and Yokohama, teeming with people, cars, and trucks. Japanese cities have all the advantages and problems found in large urban areas anywhere. There are steel and concrete skycrapers, business buildings and apartment complexes jammed close together, and houses of all sorts.

But one kind of dwelling is typical of the warmer parts of Japan, although it is not as common as it once was. That is a small, light, airy family house built with simple, traditional materials. It is put together with enormous skill, delicacy, and attention to detail.

Many of these houses are built with movable walls. You won't find walls made of massive logs or the weighty solidity of an African adobe dwelling. The walls are lightweight wood frames covered with paper or a light wood lattice. These screenlike walls slide back and forth to open up a space or close it off. In winter the thin walls are sometimes replaced by heavier ones or panels to protect against the cold, dry winds that blow in over the Sea of Japan from Siberia.

This kind of lightweight Japanese house is practical and works well in the particular climate where it is found. But there is another reason it is built this way. The Japanese are very aware of their history and cultural heritage. Where possible they like to continue this heritage by building in the traditional manner.

The traditional Japanese house has very little furniture. In fact it looks quite bare to the foreign visitor. The reason is that its inhabitants sit on cushions on the floor. There are no chairs, benches, end tables, or sofas. Usually, the only furniture is a low table around which the family gathers to eat.

There are no beds. A mat or quilt on the floor is used for sleeping and put away during the day. Clothing, blankets, and other household materials are folded up and placed in storage areas set into the walls.

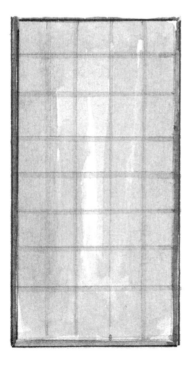

One of the special characteristics of the Japanese house is the use of wide spaces, which are opened up or closed off by sliding panels. These panels are built of wood strips and covered with thin, translucent paper.

The Japanese house is very efficient. In western homes certain rooms are used only for sleeping and only at night. The Japanese use all their rooms during the day, and can make any room a bedroom at night simply by laying out a roll of bedding called a futon.

A tatami mat, made of woven grass, is used to cover the floor of a Japanese house.

The floors are covered with grass mats. These are fairly fragile, and to protect them and keep them clean, visitors and family remove their shoes before entering the house.

To the Japanese a house is more than a place to keep out of the weather or a place to store one's possessions. The house is considered a part of the natural world, like a field or a mountain or a forest. It is regarded with appreciation, care, and sensitivity. The house is an important part of the world, and something to be made as beautiful as possible. It is a work of art.

There are, of course, many other kinds of family dwellings in Japan. There are modern houses using the most advanced ideas and materials. Many of the old-fashioned, traditional family houses use different materials and construction methods that are suited to the particular locality where they are built. Some houses have walls made of woven wooden slats covered with layers of plaster. Some are built of wood beams and boards, and there are places where stone is the common material.

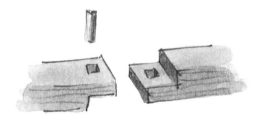

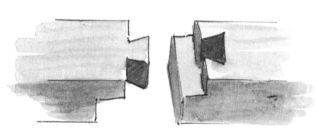

Many kinds of intricate joints keep wood beams firmly attached to one another. Nails are used infrequently.

Wood is often left unpainted for all to see, because it is so carefully and skillfully handled.

The Japanese saw cuts with a pulling motion rather than the western-style pushing motion. This allows for a narrower, sharper blade that produces a neater cut.

a Japanese saw ⟶

Gardens are an extremely important part of the Japanese house plan. Most houses have a garden that is organized very carefully and that fits in with the plan of the house. There are paths along which visitors walk as they approach the house. There are carefully chosen stones and grass and gravel areas. The garden is organized so that a particular view is seen from each part of the house. In crowded suburban areas where there isn't room for a large garden, a very small space will sometimes be planted with the most carefully chosen small flowers and miniature shrubs.

Tropical Houses

In tropical lands all over the world—Africa, the Far East, Pacific islands—a certain type of dwelling can be found. The explorer James Cook, the first Western man to set foot on many of the Polynesian islands (during the 1770's), had this to say about them: "The houses and dwellings of these people are admirably calculated for the continual warmth of the climate: they do not build them in town and villages, but separate each from the others, and always in the wood and are without walls, so that the air, cooled by the shade of the trees, has free access in whatever direction it happens to blow."

The heat and humidity of tropical climates produce abundant vegetation. There are lush, thick grasses, heavily leafed plants, and often large bamboo forests. And these, as one would expect, are the materials used for building.

A tropical house usually has a thatched roof. This roof is made from any kind of long grass. It is the commonest sort of roof and is found on primitive houses in temperate and hot climates all over the world. If the grass is arranged carefully, as shown in the drawings below, and used in many layers, it will keep out even the heaviest rains.

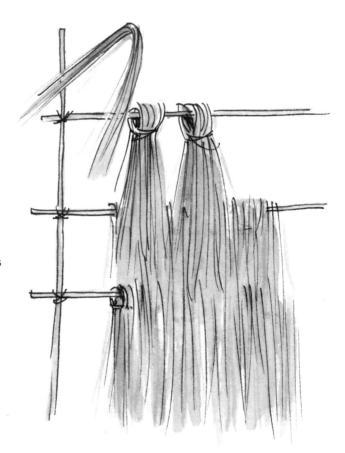

This is how a thatched roof
is put together:

The thatch itself is
simply bundles of long grass.

A framework of poles is
constructed.

Then the thatch is attached
to the framework.

The grass is bent over the
supporting pole and tied
into place. One bunch of grass
overlaps another.

Many layers of thatch will make a heavy, thick roof.

Tropical roofs usually have large overhangs so that the rain dripping off the edge of the roof won't be blown into the central part of the house. A large overhang also helps shade the house from direct sunlight.

In some places these light, open dwellings are built on poles. This serves to raise the floor well above the ground. A ladder is used to get into the house. That may seem like a lot of trouble. But it isn't such a bad idea when snakes, tarantulas, tigers, and all sorts of other disagreeable creatures are likely to be roaming about in the middle of the night. After everybody is home, the ladder is pulled up.

This raised-house-on-poles arrangement is also used by people everywhere who happen to live on swampy land or on the edges of bays, rivers, and marshes. It can be a nice experience to step out of your front door and onto a boat!

Simple shelters like this are used for cooking in parts of Africa.

Various kinds of large plant leaves can be tied to a wood frame to make a strong and watertight roof.

Dwellings that are raised high above dense foliage have a better opportunity to catch a cooling breeze.

A lofty house on stilts is not difficult to build if there is a plentiful supply of bamboo.

In tropical parts of the world bamboo is an often-used building material. It is light, very strong, and very available.

Houses in and under the Ground

There are many reasons why some people might want to live in the earth rather than on top of it. Cavemen, for example, didn't have the skills required for building a house. The best way for them to get out of the rain was to find a natural, already existing shelter like a cave. Some caves are dry and snug or can be quickly warmed by building a fire. And a cave was good protection against hungry carnivorous animals. A fire at the entrance to the cave would have kept even the fiercest animal from entering.

Another reason for building a dwelling at least partly in the ground is that it is easier to dig a hole than to build an aboveground structure. A shelter in the ground is also less likely to be blown away by strong winds or seen by marauding enemy hunters.

Partially underground dwellings have been used throughout history by people in many different parts of the world. Archaeologists have found these dwellings in Europe, Asia, Africa, and the American Southwest. Basically, they are wide, shallow holes in the ground with some kind of roof. There are many variations of this kind of dwelling, but they all have a smoke hole in common. It served to get rid of the smoke from the cooking and heating fire and was also the entrance. You would get into this kind of house like Santa Claus—by walking over the roof and climbing down a ladder through the chimney-entrance hole.

The fires used for cooking or heating were small, so they did not prevent anyone from climbing up or down through the smoke hole.

A log with notches cut in it makes a fine "staircase."

Twigs or brush can be laid over a pole framework like this.

Where tall grasses grow, a covering of thatch is often used.

The roof could be made in many ways, some of which are shown in the drawings. The American Indians in the Northwest built dwellings called earth lodges. The prairie Indians built smaller earth lodges that had earth-covered roofs on which grass grew in the summertime. From a distance these dwellings looked like grassy mounds or, in winter, snowdrifts. Only the plumes of smoke rising from the tops gave away that anyone was living there.

In northern China there are communities composed completely of underground dwellings. Light and air come in through central sunken courtyards.

Underground Ethiopian
churches, carved out of
solid rock, are still in use.

In Ethiopia there are several remarkable, complete
and elaborate churches that have been carved out of solid,
underground stone. You walk through a field, then go
down steps to enter these churches. They were built in
the seventeenth century by a group of Christians who
wanted to keep these places of worship hidden from hostile, prying eyes. Even though the windows, doors, columns, and detailing were carved directly out of solid
stone, the style is the same as that of Greek and Roman
temples, which were constructed from separate blocks of
marble. The amount of labor involved in carving these

structures is almost unbelievable: They took thousands of people many years to complete.

Today some architects are designing buildings that in principle are not very different from the primitive in-ground shelters described here. The theory is that a house built in the ground will be sheltered from bad weather. Heat contained in the ground will also help reduce heating costs. Light and ventilation can be obtained with skylights. Solar collectors can provide power for heating water. If the house is built on the side of a hill, this kind of design can provide the snug warmth and security of the earth as well as light, air, and a view facing down the hill.

The earth's temperature below the surface remains pretty much the same in all seasons. Therefore a shelter built underground will remain at approximately the same temperature winter and summer.

A primitive Irish beehive shelter.

Houses of Stone

In many places in the world there are no trees for lumber or clay for bricks and few animals to provide wool or hides with which to make tent coverings. However, even the most barren lands often have lots of stones scattered on the ground, and it is possible to build strong, permanent, weather-proof shelters using them.

In Ireland you can still see the remains of stone huts built in prehistoric times. They were built by primitive people using nothing but stones from the fields. These Stone Age structures are called beehive huts. They were easy to build because the stones didn't have to be trimmed or shaped by hand in any way; they just had to be somewhat flat on top and bottom. The people who built this

type of house didn't have the steel tools needed to cut stone into shapes suitable for square windows or tall doors.

The spaces and gaps between the stones were stuffed with dirt to make a snug, draft-proof enclosure that kept out the rain and kept in at least some heat from a small fire. When dirt was packed on top of the beehive hut, grass and flowers would eventually grow there, producing a good-looking, colorful wig. These rounded stone houses look very much like Eskimo igloos, although the materials used are certainly very different.

Some other ancient stone dwellings were built with a lot more care and skill than that which went into the Irish beehive huts. On top of a steep mountain in Peru are the ruins of a civilization that constructed perfectly engineered walls, terraces, government buildings, and temples of stone. Some of these stones weighed many thousands of pounds. Nobody knows how they were moved and fitted into place. And yet they are fitted together so

carefully that there isn't even room to slip a piece of paper in between adjoining stones.

These ruins are called Machu Picchu. Even though it is very difficult to get there, tourists come from all over the world to marvel at the dramatic setting and amazing stonework.

Although many buildings are made only of stone, others are made of stone plus other materials. For example, it isn't easy to make a stone roof, so wood is often used. Long, heavy wood beams that rest on top of stone walls provide a good support for shingled or thatched roofs. In England and in colonial America many houses were built this way.

When builders learned how to fire clay and make bricks, they often used them with stone. The house in the illustration below had large blocks of stone at the corners for strength and rigidity. These stone corners are called *quoins*. Plain bricks were used for the rest of the walls. Bricks are not very expensive, so when cost was a consideration they were often used. A piece of limestone, marble, or granite takes a good deal of time and effort to cut into shape and is bound to be a lot more costly.

———— The ruins of Machu Picchu.

Stone blocks are used for the corners of this building and also over windows and doors. Fired-clay bricks, which are much cheaper and easier to obtain, are used everywhere else.

The early builders used long, heavy stone blocks like this to span window or door openings. Any slab that serves this purpose is called a lintel, and it can be made of wood, steel, or any other suitable material.

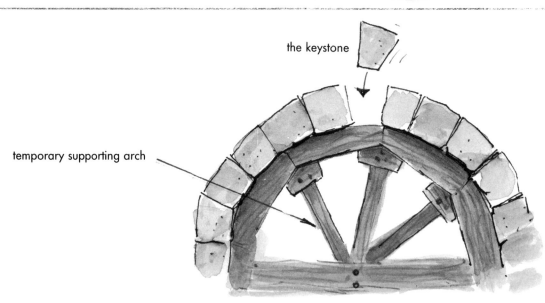

the keystone

temporary supporting arch

When stone is used to make a ceiling, it has to be positioned in the form of an arch or a curve. While the stones are being put into this kind of arch, they need a temporary support. You couldn't very well cement or glue one block of stone onto another to form a ceiling. A wooden support can temporarily hold the stones in place while the arch is being formed. Finally, when the last stone, called the keystone, is put in place, all the stones can lean against one another and the arch becomes self-supporting. Then the temporary support can be removed.

68

When builders, masons, and quarrymen become skilled at their crafts, stone became the basic building material for all kinds of elaborate structures as well as the simple one-family house. Stone was eventually used for cathedrals, royal palaces, viaducts, and elegant homes for wealthy townspeople.

Geodesic Domes

The geodesic dome is very different from the other shelters described in this book. It has a modern, technical design, which the other dwellings do not. However, because it uses few materials and is easily constructed when small in scale, it has become popular with many young people who have imagination, energy, and not much money. It is a "sophisticated-primitive" type of shelter—if such a thing is possible! Some small geodesic domes have been built for use as greenhouses, storage shelters, and summer guesthouses. Larger geodesic domes are carefully engineered, using high-tech materials such as aluminum, plastics, and prefabricated steel parts.

The geodesic dome principle was developed by the brilliant scientist and inventor Buckminster Fuller. The purpose of the geodesic dome is to get the greatest strength and rigidity with the least amount of material. A geodesic dome is a little like part of a ball. But the surface of this "ball" is built up of many small triangular shapes. The size and position of these triangles in a large dome is worked out with a great deal of care and complicated mathematics. The idea is to spread out the roof load evenly so that no heavy beams, girders, or support columns are needed.

The principles of the geodesic dome can be best understood with a few drawings of geometric shapes. The most familiar house is based on the shape of a cube. The cube form is quite suitable for the wood-beam-and-plank construction that most builders know how to do. But this kind of building is very heavy and requires a lot of material and fairly skilled carpentry. A stronger structure using lightweight materials can be put together more easily using simple triangular shapes.

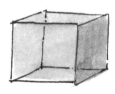

The cube is the basic shape used for many houses.

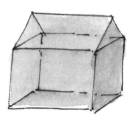

Three triangular shapes leaning against one another make a very strong structure. Here a fourth triangle makes a floor.

The drawings below show the various kinds of structures that use triangles. The simplest is a four-sided form called a tetrahedron. An eight-sided form is called an octahedron. Twenty sides gives us an icosahedron.

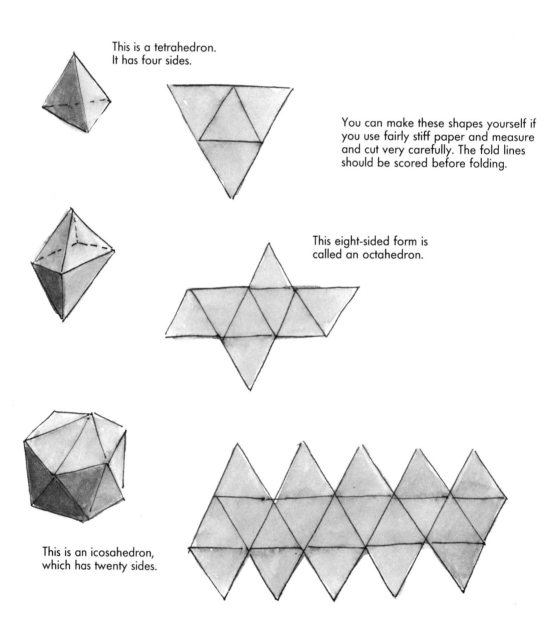

This is a tetrahedron. It has four sides.

You can make these shapes yourself if you use fairly stiff paper and measure and cut very carefully. The fold lines should be scored before folding.

This eight-sided form is called an octahedron.

This is an icosahedron, which has twenty sides.

Don't be alarmed by the tongue-twisting names. *Hedron* means a geometrical figure that has a specified number of surfaces. The prefix tells you how many surfaces. For example, *octo* is Latin for eight. Put that together with *hedron* and you have a word for an eight-sided geometrical form—an octahedron!

The icosahedron is the form most frequently used for geodesic domes. In actual practice, however, in large constructions the triangular shapes are broken up into smaller triangles. By doing this, the pieces making up the dome can be kept smaller and more manageable.

The domes are made as parts of a sphere. Some are three-quarter spheres. Some are smaller, depending on their purpose. The United States Army has been using large, three-quarter-sphere domes for years, to house a series of radar antennas in Canada. They are called radomes and have lasted through many Arctic winters.

This is a radome, used to house a radar antenna.

Lightweight geodesic domes have been designed and built so that they can be easily moved by helicopter from one location to another. These domes are thirty feet in diameter and intended for use as small-plane hangars.

Because a geodesic dome is relatively lightweight and the weight is distributed evenly over a large area, it is possible to cover huge spaces with them. Many large convention halls, exhibit halls, and storage spaces have been enclosed in this way. Buckminster Fuller even made plans for covering an entire city with a geodesic dome so that snow and rain could be kept out. Air-conditioned comfort in all seasons!

Here a geodesic dome has
been raised above the ground.

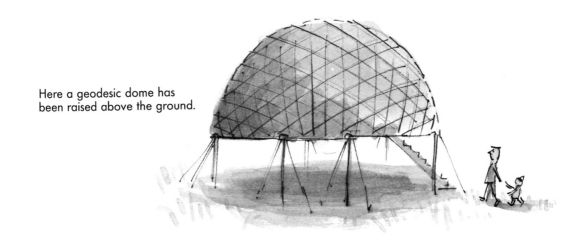

The geodesic dome can be built with
a large variety of materials. It
can also be combined with other
architectural forms.

Conclusion

Many different kinds of dwellings have been described in these pages. Some are ancient and unusual and have been discovered by archaeologists digging in strange and remote places. Some are common and still used by people living far from modern civilization. Some are included here simply because they are interesting as structures and ideas that are being or will continue to be used in modern buildings.

But the really important thing in learning about these dwellings is that they will give you some kind of understanding of the lives of the people who use or used them. And knowing and understanding other people is the basis for peaceful and enduring civilizations.